This book is for all the little boys and girls that feel unseen in this world. I see you and you are beautiful!

To my two monsters:
Jaylen, you are forever my one and only "unofficial book club buddy".
Ty, you will ALWAYS be my bacon!

Nothing in this world makes me happier than watching you two smile and laugh with each other.
I Love you MORE!!!

Written by Shannon C. Singleton and Jaylen James
Illustrated by Ujala Shahid
Edited and book designed by Bryony van der Merwe

Published in 2024
by I Rise Publishing

I RISE
PUBLISHING

www.IRisePublishing.com

ISBN: 979-8-9900501-2-9

JAYLEN & TY'S ADVENTURES

BASED ON TRUE STORIES

WHAT I LIKE ABOUT 1st GRADE

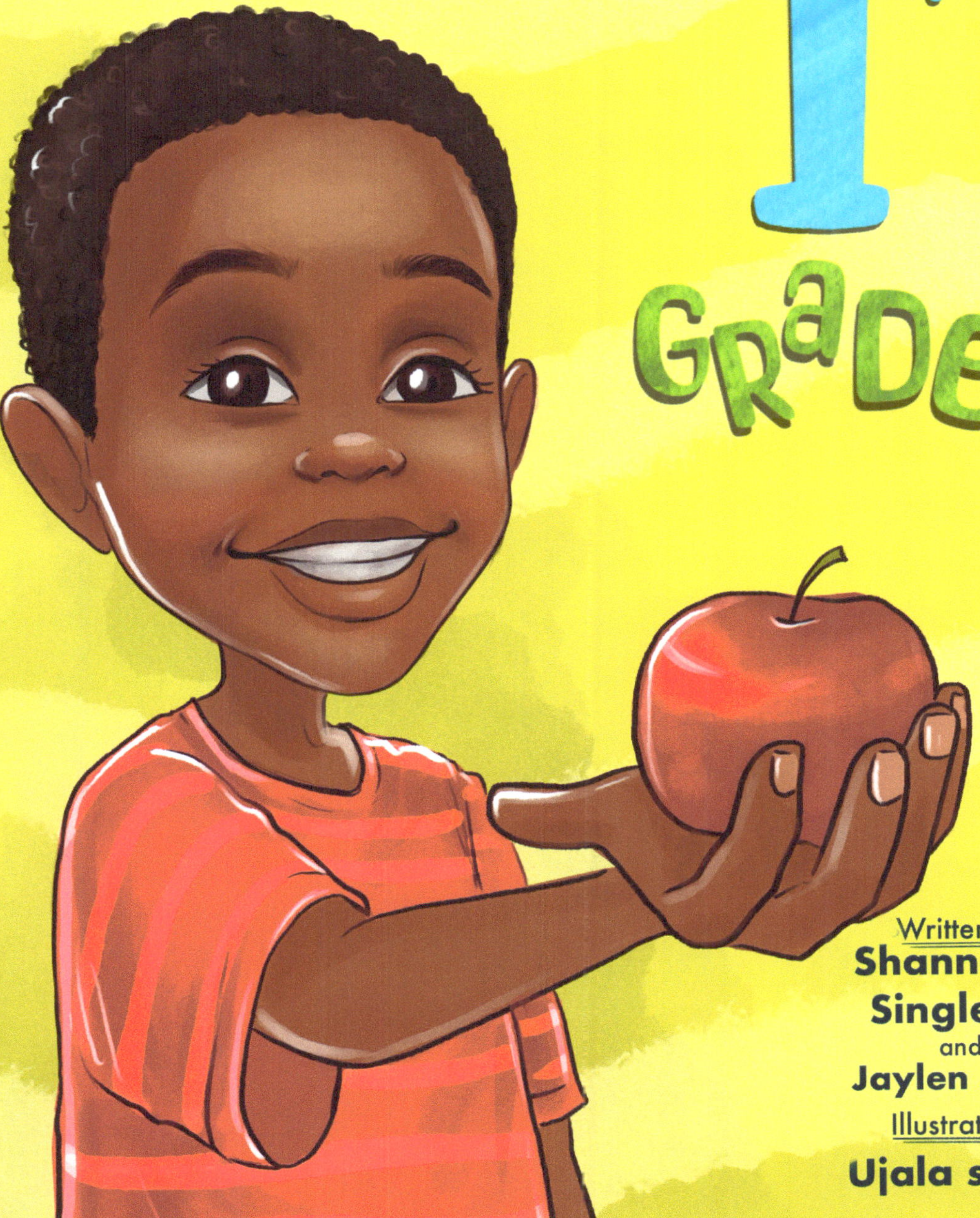

Written by
Shannon C. Singleton
and
Jaylen James

Illustrated by
Ujala shahid

My name is Jaylen, and I loved being in the 1st Grade!

Mrs. Witherington was my teacher. I was excited to go to school **each** day. I want to share some of my favorite things that happened.

I liked doughnuts with Dad! I was really **happy** that he came to school. Plus, the doughnuts were delicious.

One day, I read a **book** to the class. It was different reading to the class instead of having Mrs. Witherington read to us. I think I did a good job!

Another time, firefighters came to our school. They talked **about** how they put out fires and showed us their truck. The sirens were loud!

One Friday, Mrs. Witherington **took** us to Stone Mountain Park. I really liked petting the animals there.

In the week leading up to Halloween, I helped carve a pumpkin. It was especially fun when I moved my **hand** in the squishy parts inside it!

I really enjoyed our visit to the Yellow River Game Ranch. I like deer very much **because** they are cool.

One day, instead of regular lessons, we watched The Polar Express. We even had **hot** chocolate and candy canes!

Valentine's Day was **fun.** I passed out cards and candy to all my classmates. And I got a lot of cards and candy from them in return!

Read Across America Day was cool. Mrs. Shumake read a Dr. Seuss book to us. I love the rhyming patterns and the silly stories of Dr. Seuss.

We also took a trip to the Elachee Nature Center. It was really interesting. We touched the **animals** and learned about plants that grow in the area.

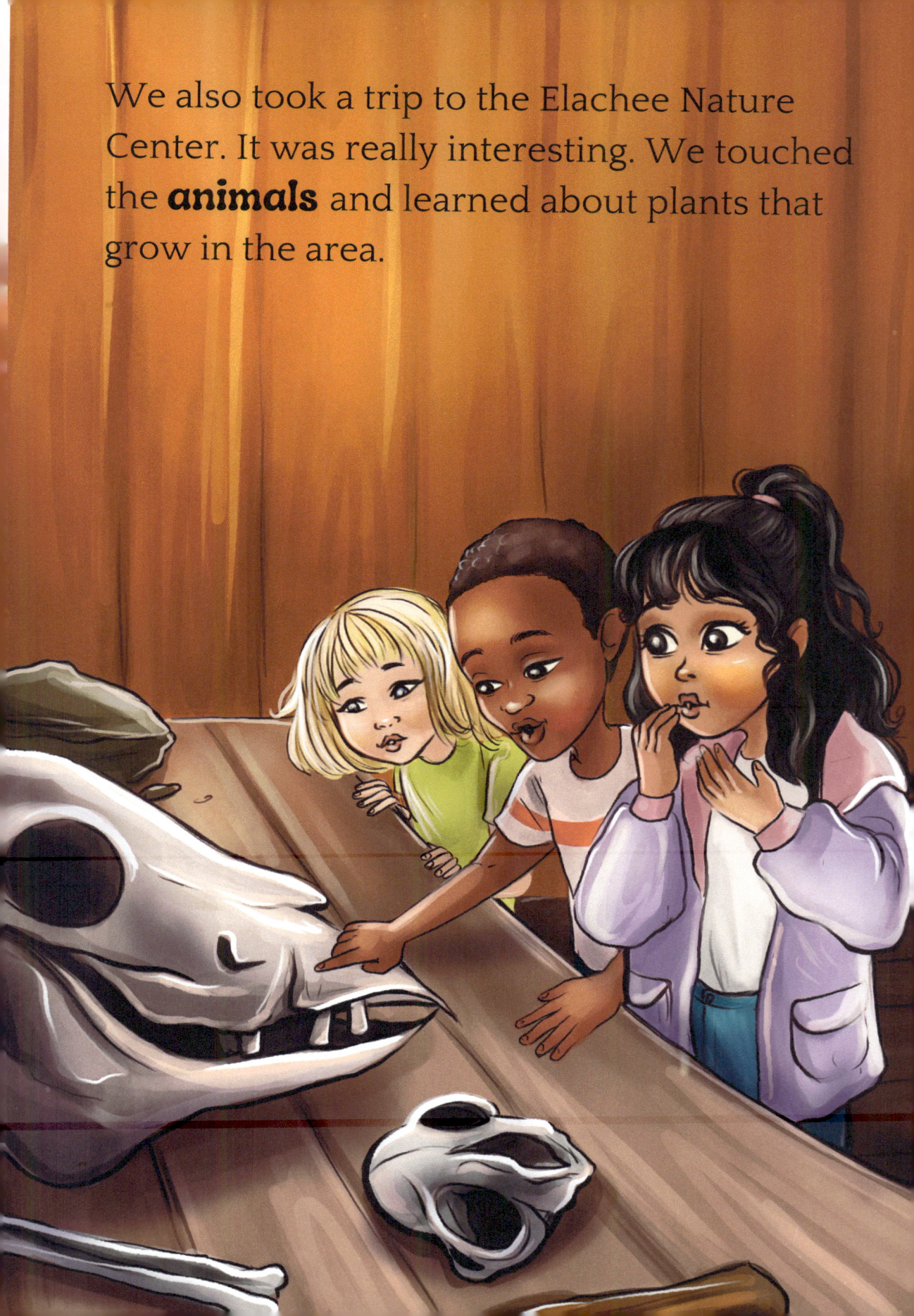

Parents were allowed to come with us to the Elachee Nature Center. I was excited that Mom was with me. We ate **lunch** together. Elachee was fun!

During art class one day, we tie-dyed **shirts** for field day.

We were going to be the Witherington **Wild** Things!

On **field** day, Kamar, Alex and I played volleyball. We hit the ball over the net.

The **other** side also hit the ball over the net.
The girls' team won.

There were a lot of games to **play.** Some of the other students even played a game with hula hoops!

I had a cone with a ball on the top.
Sometimes, I dropped the ball. Each time, I picked it up and tried again, but it still fell!

One of the things I loved the **most** about 1st Grade was playing during recess. Our playground rocked!

Man, 1st Grade **sure** was fun!

The Real Jaylen

Jaylen at 6 years old

Keep the Learning Going!

Extend the excitement of What I Like About 1st Grade with FREE guided lesson plans, printable activities, and complete Kindergarten, 1st Grade, and 2nd Grade curriculum.

Designed for families and classrooms, these ready-to-use resources reinforce foundational reading skills, build confidence, and support young learners as they grow.

Scan the QR code below to get instant access!

subscribepage.io/1Eonm3

Tie-Dye Day

Reading to the class

Visit to Stone Mountain Park

Field Day

Other Works by This Author

Jaylen & Ty's Adventures series

To learn more about each book, use the link
or QR Code below.

https://www.irisepublishing.com/books/jaylen-tys-adventures-series

About the Author

Shannon Singleton has been mesmerized by books ever since she was able to read. Her fascination with them led to her love of writing when she took Mrs. Tureau's creative writing class in 7th grade.

She is the mother of two sons, Jaylen and Ty. From a young age, Jaylen also shared her passion for reading. His ability to devour books within a day or two was amazing! Through his reading, Jaylen quickly found there weren't many books available with African American protagonists as the main character or any black characters at all. Jaylen did not see himself in the books he read.

This is something Shannon also experienced. Due to this and other events, Shannon decided to be the change she wanted to see and wrote her own book series!

She hopes that the Jaylen and Ty's Adventures Based on True Stories series allows black boys and girls to see themselves represented in a positive way really early in their lives and also for the world to see them for who they truly are!

To learn more about Shannon use the link or QR code below.
https://www.irisepublishing.com/meet-our-authors/shannon-c-singleton

Facebook

Instagram

@SHANNONCSINGLETON_AUTHOR

A Word From the Author

I appreciate you taking the time to read my book with your little one (or by yourself – no judgment here! 🙃). If you enjoyed this book, it would mean a lot to me if you took a few minutes to leave a genuine review on the platform you purchased it from. Your thoughtful feedback is very important. Thank you for your time and support!

Shannon C. Singleton

www.ingramcontent.com/pod-product-compliance
Lightning Source LLC
Chambersburg PA
CBHW041452120626
46547CB00002B/425